THE GHOST CRIB

By
Bev Clark

Edited by Sheri Jones

Cover photo: Sheri Jones and Steve Carr

Actor: Naomi Reddy

ISBN-13:
978-1539518839

ISBN-10:
1539518833

(ii)

THE GHOST CRIB
by

Bev Clark

First published in Great Britain in 2016 by **New Flight Publications**

Distributed by Amazon

For **www.scripts4stage.com**

Info@scripts4stage.com

(iii)

NEW FLIGHT PUBLICATIONS

New Flight Publications began in 2015 to promote the work of Bev Clark.

We regularly release new titles across a variety of genres.

We specialise in One-Act plays, many of which have won awards at national drama festivals.

Licences for amateur performances are available at

www.scripts4stage.com or by email at

info@scripts4stage.com

Other scripts are available on download.

From September 2016 we will be publishing the scripts in paperback via Amazon.

If you prefer a paperback script rather than a download please keep visiting our website as we will post news of each script as it becomes available.

Follow us at twitter@scripts4stage or join our face book page.

(iv)

THE GHOST CRIB
by
Bev Clark

Characters

Nathaniel Hornby a farmer (fifties)

Sarah Hornby his wife (forties)

Susannah their daughter (fifteen) a slight ailing girl.

Martha Hopkins (sixties/seventies) the village herbalist/ wise woman

Ben Kirby (almost eighteen)

Dick Slack (forties) a thief and highway man

A cottage near a village some miles from Helmsley, Yorkshire - 1760s

Note: This play could be set in any town/county and in any time from 1700-1800s. Place names may be changed. Dick and Ben's accents should be slightly different to those of the family and Martha.

The most important thing is Ben's facial make-up must be believable but at the same time grotesque.

Special effects and good lighting is necessary to create the fire scene.

(v)

SYNOPSIS

Nathaniel and Sarah Hornby have kept a secret for almost eighteen years.

Their young daughter Susannah is troubled and haunted by nightmares; they are concerned she could be possessed. They call upon Martha, a woman of medicine and herbs, who helped them in the past.

As the girl's visions become more vivid her parents begin to wonder if their past actions are to blame and they are now being punished.

When a young man arrives during a storm they are amazed by his story but he is not whom he pretends to be.

Then highwayman Slack arrives and the family are surrounded by treachery and lies but what happens next surprises them all.

Running time 50mins approx.

New Flight Publications ©*Bev Clark* *www.scripts4stage.com*

Scene 1. The cottage

It is the middle of the night. Under the blackout we hear - FX: the sound of a wooden crib creaking as it rocks; the spit of a fire which starts to crackle and burn furiously; then the terrible cry of an infant. Over this suddenly Susannah screams hysterically. Half-Light up on her in her nightgown standing petrified. Nathaniel and Sarah rush on with candles. The room is the main living area and is sparse. It shows a poor but respectable farm dwelling of 1750s. A large fireplace with a hanging pot, chairs, a table and various other props, broom bucket stools etc. There is a curtain which leads to the bedroom. Susannah sleeps on a bed near the fire with a curtain that pulls round. A door to the outside is U/S and a small window if possible.

Nathaniel: Susannah! What's wrong?

Sarah: Shush, we're here, we're here!

Nathaniel: What is it that ails the girl?

Sarah: It's the dreams!

Susannah: No! It's not a dream mother, I be awake when I hear it.

Nathaniel: What is it thee hears lass?

Susannah: I told thee father, I hear screams of a bairn.

Sarah: Why lass there is no bairn, not another house for miles around.

Susannah: But I tell thee Mother, first I hear the creaking...

Nathaniel: Creaking?

Susannah: Aye.

Sarah: Tis surely the wind in the old tree?

Susannah: No, 'tis rhythmical - like a-swaying, or a-ticking. Back 'n forth, back 'n forth...

1

Nathaniel:	There be nothing here that could make such creaking girl.
Susannah	Then I hear fire - it spits 'n cracks.
Nathaniel:	There be no fire. 'T is out... see for thyself!
Susannah:	It starts to build and leap!
Nathaniel:	Ye see it?
Susannah:	Nay, I hear the flames licking 'n hissing as if t' fire is high, fanned by a wind...
Sarah:	Nay, it can't be. How could ye hear it, if ye cannot see it?
Susannah: (frantically)	Then I hear the bairn crying and as the flames build so does its cry to a terrible scream.
Sarah:	Nay, it can't be. Nathaniel, make her stop!
Nathaniel:	Daughter, thou must say no more. 'T is just a nightmare - see there be no fire nor bairn!
Susannah:	But I hear it, I tell thee! Why won't ye listen? Why won't ye believe me?
Sarah:	Susannah, I don't know how these thoughts came into thy head, but they be wicked thoughts and ye must not have 'em. Ye must clear thy head of 'em do ye understand? (She becomes just as frantic.)
Susannah:	But I can't! I can't!

Nathaniel grabs her by the hair and with his other hand grabs a pitcher of water he drags her to where a bowl stands on the table and pours the water over her head.

Nathaniel:	Rid yourself girl! None of these thoughts.
Sarah:	Ye hear nothing do ye understand?

The girl screams and cries. Nathaniel eventually lets her go throwing her a cloth to dry herself. She sits on her bed wiping her hair whimpering.

2

Sarah: (calmer) Now hush daughter. We will say no more. I will get thee some milk and then ye must sleep. I will keep a candle on table to let you know all's well. Your father and I are only in t' other room. There is nothing to fear now. (Susannah drinks the milk)

Nathaniel: I fear I was too harsh with thee lass, but it was for thine own good. Now, try and sleep. There's milking to be done in morning and the eggs to collect. (Kindly) That be your favourite chore Susannah eh?

Susannah: Aye father.

Nathaniel: Good. Well ye rest now. Thy mother and I will sit up a bit.

She lies down on the bed and He pulls the curtain across

Nathaniel: Don't fret woman, she'll sleep now.

Sarah: (whispers) Well, what do you make of it Nathaniel?

Nathaniel: I make nothing of nothing.

Sarah: How can you say it's nothing! How does she know? I have never spoken to her of anything.

Nathaniel: It's just a dream I tell thee. Now don't read in it, more than there is.

Sarah: It's a bad omen I tell ye Nathaniel Hornby, a bad omen. She knows.
Or else some spirit is haunting her!

Nathaniel: Say nothing of hauntings in this house, woman. Speak nothing of spirits.

Sarah: That's it - we're being haunted - we're being punished.

Nathaniel: It were an accident! God's work!

Sarah: No! Not God's - it were the Devil who came here that day.

3

Nathaniel:	I tell thee for last time! We won't speak of it again.
Sarah:	And what if she dreams again tomorrow night?
Nathaniel:	If she does, then we must fetch Martha Hopkins.
Sarah:	Aye, she'll know what to do.
Nathaniel:	Aye, but none of her spells d' ye understand? I'll have no witchcraft here.
Sarah:	Witchcraft? Old Martha is no witch, she is a midwife and herbal woman and her prayers are as strong as any minister or clergy.
Nathaniel:	That's where we went wrong Sarah, we should have put more faith in that minister and said more prayers.
Sarah:	Ye think that would have done some good?
Nathaniel:	I don't think we did so good Sarah, I think God would have wanted us to do more. They call us heathens in Helmsley y' know?
Sarah:	Since when have thee worried 'bout what t' other folk say or think?
Nathaniel:	Well, I still think it best to act as God-fearing folk, if not for our sake for that of the girl. She'll be needing a husband soon so we need show our faces at Chapel more often than we do.
Sarah:	It's a long walk to Chapel and any road I know we have nothing to be ashamed of or a-feared.
	(She suddenly becomes tearful) Oh, but when I think of it, even after so many years, it seems so real as if it's happening again and I relive it.

4

(She covers her eyes and puts her head in her hands and weeps)
        Oh, I cannot bear it!

Nathaniel: Shush, now Sarah. Don't blame thyself. It was so long ago and there's nothing to be done.

Sarah: But why should it be that Susannah dreams of it?

Nathaniel: We don't know that she does?

Sarah: Do ye mean that she really does hear something?

Nathaniel: I told you, I don't know and I have no answers.

Sarah: Then we must call in Martha.

Nathaniel: Let's sleep if we can tonight. We will see what morning brings.

He takes the candle leaving the other on the table and he and Sarah exit through the curtain to their room as lights fade. Music.

Scene 2 The next morning.

Nathaniel enters from outside. He is dressed in a coat as the October weather is cold and he carries logs and twigs for the fire. Sarah is putting the bowls and cups out on the table. He goes to the fire and adds some wood so the hanging pot can be heated.

Sarah: Don't build the fire too high, there's a strong wind out there today.

Nathaniel: The pot needs to boil Sarah. Where's the girl?

Sarah: Collecting the eggs as you told her to. She'll not be long it's too cold out there to dally. I have bread from yesterday to use - I won't bake till tomorrow.

Nathaniel: I'll have no stale bread at my table woman.

Sarah: Well, we'll be luckier than most with fresh eggs and a slice of salted ham. There's many round here who'd be grateful for a slice of day-old bread alone.

Susannah enters wrapped in a shawl with a small basket of eggs

5

Susannah:	There you are mother, old Nancy's done herself proud again - biggest eggs this side of Helmsley. She's such a clever Henny.
Sarah:	Aye that she is. Every morning without fail - we'd be lost without her that's for sure. Pop them into water, we'll have' em boiled. Then there's three slices of ham left under that cloth, bring 'em to table girl.
Susannah:	Father, will ye get another pig this winter? Afore Christmas I mean.
Nathaniel:	If I get a good enough price for the sheep, we'll have more ham afore Christmas.
Susannah:	And if when you go to market you have a penny or so left might I have some ribbons father?
Nathaniel:	Ribbons? Do you think I am made of money lass? If I have any spare penny it'll be for food or more seed to sow next spring. What'll you do with ribbons girl?
Susannah:	why to wear in my hair of course - all lasses do at Christmas.
Sarah:	No not all Susannah, only those forward wenches that stay by the ale houses.
Nathaniel:	I'll have none of that for my daughter - no showing yourself off to those men in the village ... if I catch you within a mile of that place...
Susannah:	I only asked for ribbons father, I won't go nowhere near the village.
Nathaniel:	Then what do you want them for if no one sees you wear them?

6

Susannah:	Why, I'll know myself tis all…
Sarah:	The girl's soft Nathaniel - take no notice of her - now let's eat.

Sarah brings over the eggs and they all sit around the wooden table to eat. Susannah is sulking about the ribbons. FX sound of the creaking begins. Only she can hear, the parents eat their food undisturbed

Susannah:	Oh, not again. Make it stop!

The sound gets louder

Sarah:	What girl? What's the matter?
Susannah:	Can ye hear it mother?
Sarah:	What? I hear nothing!
Susannah:	The creaking!
Nathaniel:	None of that again! I told you last night.
Susannah:	There again!

The noise gets louder. Then the sound of the baby crying

O piteous! Piteous cry!

Nathaniel:	There is no sound girl! Why, you are losing your wits?
Sarah:	Nathaniel, she has never had these visions in the day before, always at night, like dreams… how can this happen?

Susannah becomes hysterical and sound gets louder

Susannah:	O the poor bairn - it will perish for sure. I must go to him.
Sarah:	Where? Where is he I can't hear him, I can't see him?

7

Nathaniel:	Stop it Sarah, there is nothing to see or hear it is all in her mind.
Sarah:	But she can hear him - I know she can! Quick fetch Martha, she is our only hope.

Susannah continues to cry and search the room by the fire

Susannah:	The cradle, I know it is here - I can hear it rocking -it must be by the fire… the flames are getting higher - see!

SFX of flames crackling/ leaping

Sarah:	Nathaniel! Look the flames! They grow higher!
Nathaniel:	Women, I will put them out - you go for Martha!

A shadow/projection of a rocking crib appears on the wall by the fire - Susannah screams out

Susannah:	Ahh! See! See! The cradle's on the wall!
Sarah:	Nathaniel - it must be true!

Susannah suddenly faints. Nathaniel runs to her

Nathaniel:	Sarah go now quickly! I will look to the girl. Fetch Martha!

Sarah is shaken but grabs a shawl and runs out of the door whilst Nathaniel picks up the girl and carries her to the bed. The vision of the cradle fades and disappears. Susannah is now whimpering and he strokes her head and sooths her. Lights fade.

New Flight Publications   ©*Bev Clark*   *www.scripts4stage.com*

Scene 3   An hour later

LX up on the same. Martha Hopkins has arrived. She is pulling the curtain across Susannah's bed. Nathaniel and Sarah are waiting for her to speak. They are nervous.

Martha: No doubt she will sleep now for a while. This business has drained the little strength she possessed.

Nathaniel: By business, what do you refer to Martha?

Martha: Why, spirit business Nathaniel, surely it is clear to thee what has taken place?

Nathaniel: Spirits? No, it must be something else - a fever? The girl ails tis all!

Sarah: I told you Nathaniel she knows something of what took place, or else she is haunted.

Martha sits by the table and pours herself some milk from the pitcher

Martha: Are you both sure that you have never uttered one word of what passed here that day?

Nathaniel: Of course we are sure.

Martha: Perhaps she overheard you when the two of you were talking, thinking she was asleep?

Sarah: No, never.

Martha: Why then if she has never picked up on anything her imagination could run wild with, I can only surmise we are dealing with some kind of haunting.

Sarah: Dear God! Are we to be punished? Tortured still? Is not our grief, pain enough?

Nathaniel: We should have confided in the Minister that day instead of you Martha. God must be displeased.

Martha: Ha! You think it is God that sends the spirit to haunt

New Flight Publications   ©*Bev Clark*   *www.scripts4stage.com*

	a young girl? Why would he do that? Tell me Nathaniel Hornby, why would our dear Lord do that?
Nathaniel:	Because, the child never had a Christian burial. Not with a proper minister!!
Sarah:	Think you the spirit is sent by... something else?
Martha:	Sarah, I want you to think. Remember back all those years ago - did ye tell me everything that happened?

Sarah tries to remember but she is confused and emotional

Sarah:	I were baking here by t' table... it were a cold day, even colder than today, so I put more wood on fire to make it warmer... the baby... Benjamin... were asleep in the crib.
Martha:	And where exactly was the crib?
Sarah:	Martha, ye know where, it always were hanging here.

She points to where the shadow/picture was.

Martha:	And Nathaniel, where were ye?
Nathaniel:	For pity sake old woman, you know where I were - out in t' field!
Sarah:	I needed some herbs for my cooking and went out to fetch 'em and then ...
Nathaniel:	Then the wind got up, blew open the door and fanned the fire - we know this, we went over it a hundred times almost eighteen year ago and a million times since -what good is this doing Martha?

New Flight Publications   © *Bev Clark*   *www.scripts4stage.com*

Martha:	Young Susannah, is a particularly sensitive child. Why, I remember the day she was born, exactly three years to the day since Benjamin were born.
Nathaniel:	Aye, they shared the same birthday what of it?
Martha:	You have never told of her of her brother, or the tragic circumstances of his death, nothing of the fire that consumed him? Yet she holds some affiliation to him - as if his little lost soul is calling out to her. She is the innocent in the house. Girls of her age - too old to be called child, too young to be called woman, can be very open to the calling of spirits and such like.
Sarah:	Martha, are you saying the spirit of my dead boy is still 'ere in this house?
Martha:	What other explanation is there Sarah?
Nathaniel:	I don't hold with talk of spirits ...but even if that could be possible... what might happen next? Is our Susannah in danger?
Sarah:	Are we all in danger?
Nathaniel:	If that was the case why has this not happened afore? Why have we lived here - the three of us - with no sign of no spirits and then this happens now?
Martha:	I would reckon something is about to happen, this might be a forewarning of something even more...
Sarah:	More what? Frightening?
Martha:	You must prepare yourselves my dears, Susannah may have been chosen...
Nathaniel:	Chosen? I am going to speak with the Minister, tell him what's happening, he'll know what to do.

He goes to leave

New Flight Publications   ©*Bev Clark*   *www.scripts4stage.com*

Martha:	Hornby, you'll have a wasted journey. The Minister was called to Helmsley on urgent business this morning, he'll not return afore tomorrow evening, so best you go about your daily business and let the girl rest. I will return tomorrow with a potion to help her sleep at night.
Nathaniel:	Potions! We'll none of your witchcraft Martha.
Martha:	Witchcraft! Is that what you call it? Why then were you so quick to accept my help when you were sick last winter with the fever? If you think I am a witch then best you seek advice somewhere else, Sarah I will take my leave of you now and may the Lord watch over this house.
Sarah:	Martha, don't go we need you here!

Martha continues to leave and exits

Nathaniel:	Ah, let her go Sarah. Good riddance Mother Hopkins! We will wait for the Minister to return. Now, I have work to do and if the girl wakes say nothing of what the old witch said, understand woman.
Sarah:	But Nathaniel.....

He is gone. She sits and cries. Lights fade

New Flight Publications   © *Bev Clark*   *www.scripts4stage.com*

Scene 4

The same: That evening.

The sound of wind and rain outside. Sarah and Nathaniel are sat by candlelight. He is counted coins on the table. She is sewing. Susannah is asleep behind the curtain.

Sarah: It's good she be peaceful tonight. The rest will nourish her.

Nathaniel: Aye, leave her to her slumber.

Sarah: She's had no supper though. She may wake with hunger.

Nathaniel: Let's just wait and see Sarah. She's no appetite at the best of times.

Sarah: So, is there enough money to get us a pig then?

Nathaniel: Aye, there is.

He puts coins into a purse and then hides in a chest or jar on table

Sarah: Then see ye get her a ribbon for Christmas Nathaniel - it'll cheer the girl's heart.

Nathaniel: Perhaps I will...

Sarah: (smiling) ...and see if you can make it a red one?

He gives a half-hearted smile in agreement as there is a loud frantic banging on the door. He jumps up to answer it

Sarah: Who on earth is knocking so late?

Nathaniel: Who's there?

(Ben's voice off) Please Sir, May I trouble you for a moment, I am lost on the road Sir.

Sarah: You best open the door Nathaniel.

New Flight Publications ©*Bev Clark* *www.scripts4stage.com*

Nathaniel unlocks the door and opens slowly

Nathaniel: Your name sir?

(Ben's voice off)   Kirby sir, Ben Kirby I am a stranger to these parts but the storm is bad and I only require a shelter until it passes.

Nathaniel: Aye well, you best step in for a while.

Ben Kirby enters he has a cloak and hood sheltering him which is wet from the storm. We see his profile open to view but the upstage side of his face is covered by his hood. He is young, almost eighteen, but assured

Ben: Thank you most kindly Sir. I am afraid I am not local to these roads. I lost my way in the storm, I am on my way to Helmsley. Tis the most frightful night.

Nathaniel: Aye, not the night for travelling.

Sarah: Please, come and warm thyself. Ye be drenched young man.

Nathaniel: Ye would have been wiser to wait 'til morning for such a journey.

Ben: Thank ye m' am. I fear I was too eager to get to my destination.

Nathaniel: What could be so important in Helmsley?

Ben: I have an uncle there who is unwell... well by all accounts dying sir and I meant to make it to him in time to... you understand my meaning... I fear I shall be too late.

Nathaniel: Well, rest a while -the storm may pass. Did you have no means by which to travel?

Ben: No sir, I am apprentice to a bootmaker ...but I do believe my uncle will have bequeathed something to me and...

Nathaniel: Ah, now I see the reason for your haste...

Ben: No, sir please do not misunderstand my intention...

14

Sarah:	Well, take off your cloak you will not dry like that.

Ben (*hesitantly.*) Thank you m'am but I prefer to keep my hood on if you don't mind.

Sarah:	In the house?
Ben:	Please understand, I wouldn't want to alarm you good people...
Nathaniel:	Alarm? What does thou mean?
Ben:	I have an affliction... a skin complaint... since I was a child. Strangers often find it hard to look upon me. There is nothing contagious you understand...
Sarah:	Why, ye poor young man... but please do not be a-feared ...we will not judge thee.
Ben:	I am afraid you may find me quite repulsive m' am - People often cannot look upon me without thinking me grotesque.

Susannah has stirred and now appears from behind the curtain

Susannah:	Mother?
Sarah:	Oh, Susannah. Did we wake you? Don't fret lass ...just a young lad sheltering here from the storm... ye try to sleep now!
Susannah:	I am thirsty.
Nathaniel:	Get the girl some milk Sarah. Sir, will ye take some ale?
Ben:	Aye I will. Thank you.
Susannah:	What is your name sir?
Ben:	Ben, Ben Kirby miss...
Susannah:	Benjamin?

Susan and Nathaniel look at each other

Ben:	Yes, but no-one has called me that since I was a child.

15

Susannah:	It is a good name.
Sarah:	Why lass, all this about a name? - It's just a name and none of your business as to whether it is good or not.
Susannah:	Why do you not take of your hood sir?
Ben:	I was explaining to your mother miss, I am better covered from the view of ladies such as yourselves, I am sure the sight of my affliction would make you both a-feared. I am afraid I am an abomination in the eyes of others.

He is emotional at this

Nathaniel:	Sir, Let me see …I will not remark on what I see but answer me this …have you been wounded or attacked by another?
Ben:	No sir. I was born this way.
Nathaniel:	Then let me see.

He goes close to Ben and slowly removes his hood. He looks first in disbelief and then in pity

	Well sir, it is not as bad as I feared…
Ben:	You are kind to say so sir, but all my life people have turned their heads from me and chosen not to speak with me. Many think because of this birthmark I must also be stupid, an imbecile, a half-wit….but I assure you sir, I have a brain… and a heart.
Susannah:	May I see you sir?

Ben turns to the light so both Susannah and Sarah now see that one side of his face is covered in a grotesque birthmark that disfigures him

Sarah:	Why, you are afflicted indeed sir…and I am sorry for your pains.
Ben:	Why, I have no pain m' am except the pain from the looks of others but there is no pain to my skin.
Susannah:	How did it happen?

16

Nathaniel:	Do not bother the young man with your questions Lass.
Ben:	It's no bother sir. My father told me I was born like this.
Sarah:	And how did your mother cope?
Ben:	My mother died at the moment of my birth.
Sarah:	So, you're father has reared you?
Ben:	No, my father left me with a cousin of his - the bootmaker I am apprenticed to. He was a soldier in the King's regiment so was always away. He did visit us from time to time.
Sarah:	Did you have no -one else, a brother or a sister?
Ben:	No ma' am it was just me.
Nathaniel:	Well, you were lucky at least that your relation took you in.
Ben:	Perhaps Sir… but I am treated as a servant, not as family. I am not allowed to sit at table with them to eat. I work long hours without another's company …
Nathaniel:	But you say you are going to see your dying uncle…
Ben:	My mother's uncle - I knew nothing of his existence until I received a letter inviting me to visit… I was not allowed to go, Cousin Jacob said I could not be spared but when a second letter came telling me of his illness, then the master said I could have three days. One day to travel there, one to stay and one to return.
Nathaniel:	But if, as you say, your uncle leaves you some inheritance then you will need not return?
Ben:	I doubt there will be enough for that, perhaps a few pounds to be given to me when I reach my maturity… the letter was from his solicitor - a Mr Matthew Dandridge .

17

He takes out a letter from beneath his cloak and holds it but does not open it and then returns it again.

Sarah:	When will you reach your maturity Mr Kirby?
Ben:	Not for another three years! I will be eighteen on 23rd January

Sarah and Nathaniel suddenly stare at each other.

Nathaniel:	You say you were born eighteen years ago on that very day?
Ben:	Yes. I was. That very day - what of it?
Nathaniel:	Nothing.
Sarah:	The very day?
Ben:	Yes. Is there some significance?
Sarah:	Tell me Mr Kirby - Benjamin - do ye know anything about the circumstances of thy birth?
Nathaniel:	Sarah! No leave thy questioning woman.
Sarah:	Nathaniel, please I need to know. Martha said that something may happen - this could be a sign.
Nathaniel:	A sign? How can it be a sign? A stranger shares a birthday with...
Susannah:	Who father?
Nathaniel:	No-one you would know lass.
Sarah:	Please Mr Kirby - do you know anything of thy birth and thy poor mother's death.
Ben:	Only what my father told me and old Bessie, the midwife who lived next door. The day was cold and windy.
Nathaniel:	Aye, well it were end of January.
Ben:	Yes, but my mother complained of the heat.

18

Nathaniel:	Aye, well most women who are about to give birth do I warrant.
Ben:	Bessie said that at the moment of my birth -a great storm arose so much the wind blew open the door of the room.
Sarah:	A wind you say... the same as here that day.
Susannah:	You remember the day mother why?
Sarah:	Shh! Lass - go on boy...
Ben:	Old Bessie said my mother was screaming, hallucinating with the pain. She believed she was in a cauldron being burnt as a witch...
Sarah:	God preserve us!
Ben:	And then I was born and when Bess saw me she said I looked as if I had been burned in the cooking pot, scalded by the water.
Nathaniel:	Dear Lord! What terror have you brought among us?
Ben:	And then as Bess lay me on my mother's breast - she calmed a while and said "Here he is little Benjamin!"
Sarah:	And then?
Ben:	Then Bess said she heaved a great breath and with her eyes cast to heaven - she died.
Sarah:	And what time of day was this- did she tell ye that?
Ben:	Why, it was in the morning I think just before mid-day.
Sarah:	Nathaniel, this can be no co-incidence. This is some kind of omen.
Susannah:	Are you the burning babe Benjamin?
Ben:	What?
Susannah:	I see him in my dreams. I hear a woman's voice call him Benjamin as she rocks him in a cradle. I see the fire start to rise and leap at the wooden crib.

19

Ben:	I do not understand you girl, what has happened here? Why do you all stare at me so?
Sarah:	We must tell him Nathaniel ...and Susannah ... we must!
Nathaniel:	Woman! Don't stir this up...
Sarah:	Daughter, you should know. You had a brother - Benjamin. He were born exactly three years before thee - to the day. When he were but four months old he were burnt in a fire - just as you dream of ... though only God knows how, for we have never mentioned him since ye were born. The day he died was the twenty third day of January....the very day of your birth Ben... and your mother gave his name to you...
Ben:	Surely, it's just a coincidence. There must be many Benjamin's born at that time?
Sarah:	But how many are born with the scar of burns to their flesh as ye have?
Nathaniel:	What are ye saying Sarah?
Ben:	You don't believe I am...?
Sarah:	I believe ye is sent to us - my son, my Benjamin - reborn...
Nathaniel:	Woman have ye gone crazy?
Sarah:	What other explanation is there?

Susannah starts to sing a lullaby -
Rock a bye sweet Benjamin, rock a bye my boy,
Daddy's gone to market to fetch you back a toy

Sarah:	That's the song I used to sing. How does the girl know that?

20

Nathaniel:	I don't understand any of this Sarah.
Ben:	Tell me sir, what does your wife mean? Can what she says be possible?
Nathaniel:	Of course not. There is some explanation….

Sarah is now mesmerised by the idea

Sarah:	He is come, Nathaniel…our Benjamin is reborn and come again to us. Susannah has found his spirit.
Nathaniel:	How can she have found his spirit - when he is here alive with us?
Sarah:	I don't know, but it's a miracle. God has sent him back to us. Benjamin my son!
Ben:	Can you love me as a son with this disfigurement?
Sarah:	I could love you whatever my son. We will not judge you here. I have been living in the dark but Susannah your sister opened the door for ye to come back to us.
Nathaniel:	Sarah! Stop this! What are ye saying? Only the Lord can be risen from the dead. This Ben is not our Ben! Our little Ben is gone.
Sarah:	I believe the Lord has sent us a miracle for all our suffering and now after all these years he has found his way back to us - what other explanation can there be?
Nathaniel:	Sarah, listen to me. Even if he were to be reborn by some miracle - why would the Lord leave him with someone else far from us for eighteen years? Why would he not send him back straight away?
Sarah:	Why it's obvious - to punish us, to punish me, I were such a bad mother leaving him unattended by the fire…

21

Nathaniel:	And his face? Why would the good Lord do that to him?
Sarah:	But perhaps it wasn't the Lord who did that... yes perhaps the Devil wanted him and took him and did that to him... but the Lord has saved him and led him back...and ....
Nathaniel:	Sarah this is madness!

Ben suddenly becomes strange as if in a trance. He looks at the fire and the place where the crib would have been.

Ben:	Oh! I remember!
Nathaniel:	What do you remember?
Ben: *(dramatically.)*	The flames from the fire!
Sarah:	Yes! Yes!
Ben:	My crib hung here I can remember the rocking...
Nathaniel:	Bairns can't remember being that young- how could ye?
Ben:	But I do. I remember the song... *(He begins to sing)* *Rock a bye sweet Benjamin, rock a bye my boy,* *Daddy's gone to market to fetch you back a toy*
Sarah:	Ye see he remembers my song...
Nathaniel:	But Susannah was singing that before...

Now both Susannah and Ben sing it over rocking back and forward in a kind of trance

Sarah:	I don't care what you say Nathaniel, Martha was right - we are blessed!
Nathaniel:	I will not stay here to witness this Sarah, I will go all the way to Helmsley to get the minister if I have to but I will get to the bottom of all this once and for all.

New Flight Publications   *© Bev Clark*   *www.scripts4stage.com*

Sarah:	You have no faith Nathaniel, that's your problem come pray with me, let's give thanks…
Ben:	Mother, I know you are my mother now I have dreamt of your face …I never knew who the strange woman in my dreams was, but now I do…Father, Father …
Nathaniel:	Don't call me that! I don't know who ye are but ye are not my son - he is dead and buried in the ground. I put him there myself!
Ben: *(with passion.)*	That was his body you buried but his spirit entered this body, for as he died I was born and I know now why I was sent here this night…. I know why my parents called me Benjamin… they were told by God….
Nathaniel:	It's impossible!
Ben:	Then how do you explain this *(he points to his birthmark.)* Surely you can't believe this is just a co-incidence?
Nathaniel:	What of thy other family - thy cousins, thy dying uncle?
Ben:	They have never loved me… I have never belonged there…I always knew…
Nathaniel:	What did ye know boy?
Ben:	In my dreams I would see a cottage… like this with three chairs at a table like this. I never saw the faces apart from that of the woman, who I now know was my mother. There was the shadow of a man but I never saw his face and there was a small child, a girl playing on the floor and she had ribbons in her hair - red ribbons…I believe the man was you Nathaniel and the child was Susannah.

23

Susannah:	I have no red ribbons.
Sarah:	But ye were to have them child. I told thy father to fetch 'em from market for ye only just today... how did he see us in his dreams Nathaniel?
Nathaniel:	We don't know he did.
Sarah:	Ah, do ye have no faith man? Mr Hornby, ye are a heathen!
Nathaniel:	I am no heathen woman and I have the sense the good Lord gave me and I need to clear my head and think on all this!

He storms out into the raging storm. Sarah holds Ben to her and rocks him with her eyes up to heaven but Susannah stands watching them both.

Sarah:	Praise to God. My son is returned. My son, my boy, my Benjamin!
LX FADE	

SCENE 5. The next morning.

Susannah and Ben are seated at the table whilst Sarah makes breakfast.

Ben:	I should be leaving for my uncle's soon. I must still make that journey.
Sarah:	But why? There is no need for you to go.
Ben:	Mother... forgive me it sounds strange to call you that....
Sarah:	But you must Benjamin, you cannot call me Mrs Hornby.
Ben:	Well only here in the house, other people may think it strange if they overhear it. As I say, if I should visit my uncle and if I should receive a small gratuity it will help you and Nathaniel ...

Sarah:	Father you mean… He will see truth I am sure…
Ben:	Well… if you really do mean me to stay here?
Sarah:	Of course we do. As soon as he returns I will speak with him. We can convert some space in the barn to make thee a room of a kind. Ye can't sleep in a chair every night can ye?
Ben:	Would that be possible? Would it not be expensive? My uncle's money could help…
Sarah:	We have enough money put by - Nathaniel has not yet been to market this month so we have the money for the pig.
Susannah:	Mother! We need the pig.
Sarah:	We can manage without Susannah, a brother and son for Christmas is far more important. Now we should all go off to the village this morning I need to get flour to bake bread.
Susannah:	All of us? Won't they think it odd ma, for him to be with us?
Ben:	Yes. They will. Besides they will stare at me.
Sarah:	We can say ye are a visiting relation.
Susannah:	Mother that's a lie!
Sarah:	It is not - he is a relation is he not?
Ben:	But no one will believe us. They will think you mad - I would prefer to stay here please. Besides I am tired. I could write to my uncle and say I am delayed for a day or two…
Sarah:	Very well. Susannah and I will not be long.

They start to put on capes/cloaks and Sarah whispers to Susannah whilst Ben continues to eat

New Flight Publications   © Bev Clark   www.scripts4stage.com

Sarah:	Lass, whilst we are out we must visit Martha and tell her what has happened here. She will know what to do. Come now. Goodbye Benjamin. We will not be long.

They exit

Ben looks around the cottage as if he is searching for something. After a while he goes to the door looks out waiting for the women to disappear and then he whistles and leaves door on the jar. Soon Dick Slack enters.

Dick:	You took your time Kirby!
Ben:	These things can't be rushed Dick.
Dick:	Well, by the look of it your story was convincing. Where is the old man?
Ben:	I am not sure. Hornby wasn't so easy - the missus was caught like a fly in a trap almost as soon as I opened my mouth.
Dick:	And the Lass?
Ben:	She is a weird one, a bit strange. They say she hears voices and sees spirits which all kind of added to the drama if you ask me.
Dick:	So, have you found it? The stash of money. Old Barney was sure he had plenty hid away.
Ben:	I know he has some put by to spend on a pig but my guess is there is more here if we search.
Dick:	I thought, you having contact with the spirit world and such, you would be able to nose it out as easy as anything. (*He laughs*)
Ben:	Stop your jesting and help me look!

They search around the house and Dick soon finds the bag of money in the jar.

26

Dick:	There you are my beauty! A bag of silver for Jack and his boy.
Ben:	Don't call me your boy Slack.
Dick:	Ah, but you are. Wasn't it old Dick Slack that saved you from that travelling show? Just a boy - a little freak!
Ben:	Shut up Dick! I am a man now and after this job I want an equal share of any pickings.
Dick:	Equal? We'll see about that. This job only happened because old Dick keeps his ears and eyes open. If I hadn't overheard that story about a baby being burned in a fire from some loose tongued old witch in the village, you could never have pulled it off. You should take to the stage, you must be a right little actor!
Ben:	Ha! Mister Jack Kirby impersonator of the dead …except I would have to wear a mask wouldn't I? No matter how clever I am Dick, I can never be anything than a man in a mask or hidden under a cloak.
Dick:	You getting sentimental Jack or should I call you Ben?
Ben:	This woman, Ma Hornby she was prepared to love me as her son, despite my affliction.
Dick:	She wouldn't love you if she knew the truth. You have just tugged at her guilty heart strings. The old mare has been living in hope her son might be returned to her by some miracle…
Ben:	Aye and I was that miracle.
Dick:	You not going soft are you lad?
Ben:	No. But maybe I be better off here.
Dick:	After all old Dick done for you, fed you, clothed you?

27

Ben:	Only so I could do your bidding, your dirty work. Thieving and murdering.
Dick:	Look, your real parents, those travelling gypsies, they cared nothing for you and believed they were cursed in having a maimed bairn. Maybe it would have been better if you had died when you were a tot, cause after that all they did was make a living out of showing you in their freak show, when I took you... because remember they didn't want you boy, I was a good a father as I could be to you, given my circumstances.
Ben: (*Sarcastically.*)	You have a knack of making me feel so much better Dick - what life have I had? The life of a highwayman?
Dick:	Well, you've had adventure boy and food and ale and the freedom to go where you fancy...now keep looking.

They continue but Nathaniel comes in and startles them. Dick grabs his pistol from his coat.

Nathaniel:	What the..? Who the hell are you?

Dick grabs him in a threatening manner. There is a struggle. Eventually Nathaniel is dragged to the chair

Dick:	You keep yourself sat on this here chair ol' man - and you tell me where I can find your stash?
Nathaniel:	Stash? What mean you?
Dick:	Your money Hornby.
Nathaniel:	I got no money - I am a poor man.
Dick:	Ha! That's where you are lying ...if you have no money - what's this? So where's the rest?
Nathaniel:	That's mine you thief!

28

Dick:	Sit down! Where's the rest? Jack keep searching.
Nathaniel:	Jack is it? I suspected ye were some kind of fraud ye vermin.
Ben:	Just give him the money Hornby and you won't get hurt.
Nathaniel:	How did ye do it boy? How did ye know about our Ben? What have ye done with my wife and daughter? Where be they?
Ben:	They went to the Mill. They will be all right - just give us your money and we'll be gone before they get back.
Nathaniel:	How could ye do that to my Sarah? She believes ye are a miracle from God. But ye are from the Devil - how, how did ye know?

Sarah appears in the doorway and screams dropping the bag of flour

Nathaniel:	Sarah! Run! We are deceived - thieves, woman run!

Sarah is staring at Ben in disbelief

Sarah:	Benjamin? Son? What is happening? Who is this stranger?
Dick:	My name is of no concern to you woman. Me, and my accomplice here, are to relieve you of your money and belongings.
Sarah:	Thieves?
Dick:	Ha, ha that we are!

(He is still holding Nathaniel down in the chair)

Nathaniel:	See woman - behold your miracle is nothing but a trickster and surely he is the Devil's man. How these two know of our tragedy and how they have

29

	turned it to their advantage only that... boy... can tell us... I warned ye...
Sarah:	But ye let him in Nathaniel, ye believed he were an honest traveller on his way to see his uncle... is that not true either?
Ben:	No. I am no apprentice to any bootmaker - only to this gentleman.
Sarah:	And is thy name not Benjamin ...?
Ben:	He calls me Jack - I never knew my real name.
Sarah:	And thy poor dead mother and thy soldier father what of them?
Ben:	I was born to travelling folk - Gypsies, until he, took me from them.
Sarah:	And thy face? Thy affliction?
Ben:	I was born like this but no-one knows why. They believed I was cursed.
Nathaniel:	Sarah, we don't need to know who he is or his history -only how he knew about ours?
Ben:	Give us all you have then and I will make sure no harm comes to you... and I will give you satisfaction to know how I came to you - just give him the money or I fear for your lives.
Dick:	Now, now let us not get dramatic young Jack! As if I would do harm to these good folks.
Ben:	I know you Dick - promise if they give us everything, we can leave them unharmed!
Dick:	Why should I?

He grabs Sarah and pushes her down on the other chair threatening her with pistol

New Flight Publications   *©Bev Clark*   *www.scripts4stage.com*

	Now, where are your other valuables?
Nathaniel:	Don't hurt her! In there, behind the curtain where the girl sleeps you'll find a box... there are a few treasures...
Sarah:	No Nathaniel - it's all we have!
Ben:	Where is Susannah? Why was she not with you?
Sarah:	She stayed with Martha, she's helping her *(lying)* she won't be back for hours....
Dick:	Martha? Well, she must be the one responsible for all this then.
Nathaniel:	How do you mean?
Dick:	Because of her I know your story Hornby.
Nathaniel:	Martha would tell thee nothing. She'd not speak with the likes of you!
Dick:	Jack search for the box. I will take me a pitcher of ale and give them their story.

Ben searches and comes out with a small box he opens it and pulls out some letters, coins, gold chains etc.

Dick:	Not much but it will have to do.

He slurps the ale.

'T was almost eighteen year ago. A cold January day and I was running - I'd been poaching and the game-keeper was a chasing me so I jumped the wall into a cottage and found the door unlocked. I didn't know it but it were Martha's cottage... but no sooner was I in, than I heard voices approaching so I hid under table and I was then forced to listen to what followed.

31

Ben:	Dick, leave it now, we have what we came for - let us go now.
Dick:	No. they want their explanation - and I shall give it them.

Ben is agitated. He knows Dick is only telling them because he intends to kill them anyway

Dick:	So, three people were there - Martha and you Hornby and your then young wife - you Mrs! You were blubbering and nervous and in such a state…. You then tell Martha what has happened - the wind, the fire, the crib burning and you have another with you - your dead baby lady! The baby you killed!

Sarah is crying hysterically

Sarah:	It was an accident!
Nathaniel:	So you found out our secret…then why did you not use it against us then? Why come back all these years later?
Dick:	Why then it was nothing to me - a baby burned in a fire? I could not see it as anything I could turn to my advantage. It was an hour before I could make my escape and then… I was on the road travelling all the highways of England, finding young Jack here along the way some years after.
	Then a few days ago we find ourselves back here and I recall old Martha's cottage… and then in the tavern tongues are loose and wagging about the Hornby's who lost their baby and live up here with their weird daughter away from everyone else…and how old

32

	Hornby had a few pounds stashed away from his sheep... well old Dick gets to remembering all he heard that day and then I look at my boy Jack there...
Ben:	I am not your boy!
Dick:	I look at he and I gets me a plan in my head - My head is very good at plans Hornby, and young Jack is a bit of an actor - very convincing don't you think?
Nathaniel:	So it seems.
Sarah:	So, you have used the boy for your own account?
Dick:	Make no mistake woman, Jack is as black-hearted as I. He was after your money the same.
Sarah:	Tis you who have made him black-hearted then. Ben - Jack - you may not be my son... I realise I have been deceived and I am a stupid woman for believing in miracles...but boy, ye are not like him, ye could be a good man given a chance.
Ben:	Chance? What chance would the world give me when I look like this? All I have is shadows for company...
Dick:	The boy knows where he is best off - he could never live a normal life.
Ben:	Sometimes I think I would be better off dead.

Whilst Sarah has been talking to Ben and Dick counting over his takings Nathaniel sees his moment He jumps on Dick and takes his pistol - a struggle. Sarah then grabs the jug and hits Ben over the head. He is startled but not knocked out.

Nathaniel:	Quick Sarah get the rope we will tie them to the chairs!

New Flight Publications   ©Bev Clark   www.scripts4stage.com

Nathaniel puts two chairs back to back and Dick and Ben are tied to chairs. Whilst Sarah nervously hold the pistol on them. As this is happening Susannah appears.

Susannah: Mother! Father!

Nathaniel: Don't be a-feared Lass! We have caught as a couple of thieves and con-men.

Sarah: O Susannah, our Benjamin is not our Benjamin but some trickster and robber.

Susannah: What has happened here mother?

Sarah: Don't think of it now - just run to the village and get help.

But Susannah isn't listening; instead she can hear the faint sound of fire crackling and the wind.

Nathaniel: Why do you tarry girl? Quick run for help.

Susannah: Can you not hear it father?

Nathaniel: What?

Susannah: The wind. There is another storm coming!

Nathaniel: Stupid girl, don't bother about the weather - go!

Susannah: Mother I can hear the fire spit and crackle.

Sarah: What? The fire is out - are you mad?

As Sarah is distracted Dick makes a break and gets free from the ropes. He and Nathaniel struggle whilst Ben tries to get the pistol from Sarah but Susannah now stands in the centre of the room. The sound of a howling wind is building. The door flies open and suddenly the fire rises. It starts to burn ferociously. Then we start to hear a baby cry and Susannah begins to sing the haunting song. At this the others react and panic. Dick make a run for it. Nathaniel and Sarah are bewildered and Ben stands transfixed.

Nathaniel: Quick Sarah grab the girl we must leave - the house will burn!

34

Sarah: Susannah! Quick!

But Susannah only moves to the back where the crib appears on the wall she turns her back and as the effects grow and the chaos ensues she turns again holding a baby in her arms.

Susannah: Shhh! Little Benjamin do not cry!

Sarah: Nathaniel! Look! Look!

Nathaniel: Sarah we must leave this place she is bewitched!

Nathaniel and Sarah are overcome with flames and smoke. Susannah is unaffected. Nathaniel drags Sarah to the door.

Nathaniel: Come away woman - we cannot save her!

Sarah: No! Not my children I will not leave both my children.

Then Ben goes to Susannah and takes the child. He too, is unaffected but the fire now is intense. Sarah battles through and grabs Susannah pulling her from the flames, whilst Ben holds the baby and starts to sing the song. As the cottage burns the family escape and only Ben is left with the child until the fire rises up and consumes them both. Blackout.

Silence.

A light comes up on Sarah and Susannah seated. She is comforting the girl.

Sarah: Susannah! Child can you speak?

Susannah: They are gone mother. They will not return again.

Sarah: What has happened?

Susannah: Little Benjamin is at rest mother and so is Jack - he has found peace. They will not judge him in Heaven.

Sarah: Heaven? Could it be the boy is with our Lord, for all his wickedness?

Susannah: He is redeemed mother, little Benjamin came back to save him.

New Flight Publications   ©Bev Clark   www.scripts4stage.com

Nathaniel appears in the light

Nathaniel: We will take a new cottage… down in the village…we will start anew… and Lass, these are for thee…

He hands her some red ribbons.

Susannah: O father, red ribbons - they are beautiful. Now I can be just like the other lasses.

Slowly the lights come up again to show the debris of the old cottage. She starts singing the song - the shadow of the crib is on the wall but slowly fades and before she reaches the end of the song she stops

Susannah: I cannot remember the words mother!
Sarah: That song is done Susannah, thou art free… all my children are free.

Sarah gently rocks her daughter in an embrace whilst Nathaniel stands with his hands on their shoulders. The door is open and as the image of the crib fades bright sunlight pours in and the sound of birdsong can be heard.
Fade to Black out.

PROPS: Cooking pot, various pots pans and utensils, jug of milk and ale, broom bucket and other household things. A pistol. A basket. Red ribbons. Candles. Money pouch.

END

New Flight Publications   *©Bev Clark*   *www.scripts4stage.com*

ABOUT THE AUTHOR

BEV CLARK is a writer, director, producer and drama facilitator who lives on Wirral in Merseyside.

She has worked in theatre-related environment for most of her career mainly as a youth theatre facilitator. In 2011 she was received by Her Majesty the Queen at Buckingham Palace for her work with young people in the arts.

Bev is an adjudicator with The Guild of Drama Adjudicators (GoDA) and has written and directed youth and community theatre pieces for many organisations and theatre groups. She is also the Artistic Director of Hand in Hand Theatre - a community arts company who have won much acclaim and many awards since 2008.

In 2015 her play THE BLACK EYES, a one-act teen drama, won the Roister Doister International Play for Young People and is now published by them at www.roisterdoister.com. Also available on Amazon. A gripping production of this horror-story won through to the quarter-finals of the All England Theatre Festival (central region) in 2016.

Having written many one act plays, as well as poetry, short stories and songs, Bev is now concentrating on more writing and publishing projects. You can follow her on twitter @hihtheatre and twitter@scripts4stage

OTHER TITLES by Bev Clark

AVAILABLE ON AMAZON.

Baggage One Act two hander for women.

Make Me Invisible - Youth drama. Ensemble physical theatre.

RIP Mr Shakespeare - co-written with Keith Hill.

When the Dark Sea Cries -period drama for large female cast

The Black Eyes - teen horror physical theatre from www.roisterdoister.com and Amazon.com

Available from www.scripts4stage.com

Remembrance Day. One Act family drama NDFA finalist and AETF semi-finalist 2009

Bentley: Road to Justice. One Act Docudrama AETF semi-finalist 2011

Running out of Time One Act comedy drama with a twist

BOX One Act Theatre of the Absurd set in a psychiatric hospital

S.PA.C.E One Act two hander for women

Jessie's Tree Youth Ensemble - a family history across a century

Stealing Me - One Act comedy about Identity fraud

After The Dream - Two act modern sequel to a Midsummer Night's Dream

A life Unspoken - One Act drama. Currently available from www.lazybeescripts.com

New Flight Publications   ©*Bev Clark*   *www.scripts4stage.com*

Printed in Great Britain
by Amazon